Pterodactyl Rose

POEMS OF ECOLOGY

Books by
WILLIAM HEYEN

Poetry

Depth of Field (1970)
Noise in the Trees: Poems and a Memoir (1974)
The Swastika Poems (1977)
Long Island Light: Poems and a Memoir (1979)
The City Parables (1980)
Lord Dragonfly: Five Sequences (1981)
Erika: Poems of the Holocaust (1984) (1991)
The Chestnut Rain (1986)
Brockport, New York: Beginning with "And" (1988)
Falling from Heaven: Holocaust Poems of a Jew
   and a Gentile (with Louis Daniel Brodsky) (1991)

Anthologies

A Profile of Theodore Roethke (Editor, 1971)
American Poets in 1976 (Editor, 1976)
The Generation of 2000: Contemporary American Poets
   (Editor, 1984)

Novel

Vic Holyfield and the Class of 1957 (1986)

Pterodactyl Rose

POEMS OF ECOLOGY

by
William Heyen

TIME BEING BOOK**S**
POETRY IN SIGHT AND SOUND
Saint Louis, Missouri

Time Being Books
10411 Clayton Road
Saint Louis, Missouri 63131

Time Being Books volumes are printed on acid-free paper, and binding
materials are chosen for strength and durability.

Library of Congress Catalog Card Number: 90-72138

ISBN 1-877770-24-8
ISBN 1-877770-25-6 (pbk.)
ISBN 1-877770-27-2 (tape)
ISBN 1-877770-26-4 (tape & pbk. set)

Designed by Ruth A. Dambach
Southeast Missouri State University
Manufactured in the United States of America

First Edition, First Printing (July 1991)

Grateful acknowledgment is made to the editors of the following periodicals, in which many of these poems first appeared: *American Poetry Review* ("Fulcrum: The New Poem," "The Gift"); *The American Review* ("The Pigeons"); *Amicus Journal* ("Emancipation Proclamation"); *Bluefish* ("Deer"); *Colorado Review* ("Matrix," "The Swamp"); *Cream City Review* ("Futures"); *First Things* ("Liturgy"); *Forum* ("The Children"); *The Georgia Review* ("Birdhouse"); *Modern Poetry Studies* ("The Stadium"); *The Ohio Review* ("Trees"); *The Ontario Review* ("The Real News," "Harpoon," "Dodo," "Trident II: 720,000 Hiroshimas," "A Jar," "Looking Away," "Elmwood"); *Pennsylvania Review* ("Night Flight from England"); *Pig Iron* ("The Global Economy"); *Ploughshares* ("Pterodactyl Rose," "Stuff," "Fast Food," "Gods of Vanished Species"); *Poetry* ("The Buffalo," "Redwings"); *The Seattle Review* ("Yellowjackets").

"The Stadium" and "Off the Hamptons" appeared in **Depth of Field** (Baton Rouge: Louisiana State University Press, 1970); "The Pigeons" in **Long Island Light: Poems and a Memoir** (New York: Vanguard Press, 1979); "The Host," "Redwings," and "The Buffalo" in **The City Parables** (Athens, O.: Croissant & Co., 1980); and "Yellowjackets" in **Brockport, New York: Beginning with "And"** (Dallas: Northouse & Northouse, 1988).

William B. Ewert (Concord, N.H.) published "My Sleigh Tonight" as a holiday card in 1990.

The author would also like to thank the State University of New York College at Brockport for a sabbatical, during which this book came together in its final form.

For

Martin Booth

CONTENTS

Pterodactyl Rose

POEMS OF ECOLOGY

Harpoon

Now that blue whales are as few as two hundred,
I want the last one dead.
I need to forget them right away,
    before the last reports:
        ships stripping lost codes of flesh,

        the last calf wandering away, &, later,
    are there any left?
Before the last eye is cut out, dumped overboard,
    & floats away,
        & what it sees. Kill them now, please,

        before politics can't save them —
the fountaining overtures
the biblical jaws the blue tinge fathoms deep
    the evolutionary curves our
        predecessors' pitiful & beautiful last songs.

Liturgy

We kept building our steeples higher until
emissions streamed to thousands of miles away,
but distant lakes spit up frogspawn & fish,

so we built our steeples higher until —
though at first we couldn't tell — emissions
circled the globe to snow & rain

on us. So we built our steeples higher,
through mackerel clouds, the last chains
of food. Instead, we should have dug a hole

like a cathedral in the earth, receptacle for all
preternatural desire. Adream, we'll kneel
in pews there: flowers of stained glass above us

& censers swinging by, a choir advertising wind
tearing over our steeples higher & higher.

Dodo

Large. Flightless. No predators.
Secure on Mauritius ten million years.
Slow moving. Trusting. Ungainly
and beautiful. Eyes gray, maybe —
no one knows for sure.

Dutch sailors. Later, colonists'
clubs and dogs. The last
dodo died in 1680. Ungainly
and beautiful. Eyes pink, maybe —
no one knows for sure.

Ate the fruit of *Calvaria major*,
the dodo tree, which could not propa-
gate itself without its dodo, ungainly
and beautiful. Eyes blue, maybe —
no one knows for sure.

By 1970, only thirteen trees, the last
of their species in this world, were left. . . .
The dodo sometimes seemed to smile, ungainly
and beautiful. Eyes black, maybe —
no one knows for sure.

To germinate, the tree's seeds
needed to be crushed
in the dodo's craw. Ungainly
and beautiful. Eyes ochre, maybe —
no one knows for sure.

On other secret intricacies, it's mum,
and will be. In the British Museum,
I saw one stuffed one: ungainly
and beautiful, one socket
empty, one sewn shut.

The Pigeons

Audubon watched the flocks beat by for days,
and tried, but could not count them:
their dung fell "like melting flakes of snow,"
the air buzzed until he lost his senses.

He heard, he said, their *coo*
and *kee* when they courted, and saw trees
of hundreds of nests, each cradling two
"broadly elliptical pure white eggs."

Over mast, they swept in "rich deep purple
circles," then roosted so thick that high limbs
cracked, and the pigeons avalanched
down the boughs, and had not room to fly,

and died by thousands. Kentucky farmers
fed their hogs on birds
knocked out of the air with poles. No net, stone,
arrow, or bullet could miss one,

so horses drew wagons of them,
and schooners sailed cargoes of them,
and locomotives pulled freight cars of them
to the cities where they sold for one cent each.

When you touched one, its soft
feathers fell away as easily as a puff
of dandelion seeds, and its delicate breast-
bone seemed to return the pulse of your thumb.

Redwings

Maybe you've noticed that around here
red-winged blackbirds aren't rare,
but aren't seen often, either, and then, at distance,
banking away from roads as we pass.

But one morning, I saw a hundred,
more, feeding on seed I'd scattered
under a line of pines planted
more than a hundred years before.

Almost at rest, their feathers folded close,
only yellow wingbars
break their black bodies. But when, as they did,
all at once, they lifted, that *red* . . .

I've tried for a long time, and maybe should,
to tell you how the disembodied redwings
flared and vanished.
I've lost them in every telling.

So much for me. I could die now, anyway.
Could you? We will close our eyes
and rest, in case the blackbirds, in slow motion,
assume again the flames they are, and rise.

The Host

In the dying pond,
under an oilspilled rainbow where
cement clumped, cans rusted, and slick tires
glinted their whitewall irises,
at the edge where liquid congealed,
a lump of mud shifted.
I knew what it was,
and knelt to poke it with a wire
from the saddest mattress in the world.

Maybe a month out of its rubbery egg,
the young snapper hid,
or tried to, drew back its head,
but algae-scum outlined its oval shell,
its ridged chine diminished
toward its tail,
and I lifted the turtle
into the air, its jaws open,
its crooked neck unfolding upward.

It twisted, could not reach me.
I found out its soft, small undershell where,
already, a leech lodged
beneath its left hindleg, sucking
some of whatever blood
its host could filter from the pond, its host.
They would grow together, if the snapper lived.
Its yellow eyes insisted it would.
I gave it back to the oil sludge

where it was born, and watched it
bury itself, in time, and disappear. . . .
I'd like to leave it living there,
but churned slime above it blurs, burns,
bursts into black glare, every atom
of chemical water, rust residue, human vomit
shining in deathlight. The snapper's
bleached shell ascends the 21st century,
empty, beyond illusion.

Desoulment

Austin tried to save its treaty oak
poisoned by a follower of Satan
who wanted it dead, this disciple said.

Despite soil replacement, feedings & mistings,
a canvas canopy of stress-reducing shade,
the tree withered. Even a wizard,

allowed to try his skill, did everything he could,
but one moment, the moon above them,
his transcendental temple against the tree,

he felt its spirit leave it — as last night,
when I knelt to place my ear against our earth,
I felt its spirit leave it.

Futures

1.

I lay under the dream ark in mid-water, not swimming,
just in limbo there, heard Noah pacing
among our animals, praying for the skies to clear,
mumbo-jumbo, mutter and slur.
I knew the future, so rolled over to stare downward
where Ararat hissed and seethed.
Better off unborn, but, around me, jellyfish brains hooked
ganglia to the sea floor.

2.

In a Thames dream on fire bloodsmell I'm somewhere near
the tower bridge split
upward right angle hundreds clawing flesh reach high
portal to air the sky streaks
jerks upward explodes I fist another whose
leg breaks beneath my chest if
only for one last breath, last alive, triumphant,
what I was born for.

The Stadium

The stadium is filled,
for this is the third night the moon
has not appeared as even a thin sickle.

We light the candles we were told to bring.
The diamond is lit red with torches.
Whole sections of the bleachers begin to moan.

The clergy files from the dugouts
to makeshift communion rails
that line the infield grass.

We've known, all our lives,
that we would gather here in the stadium
on just such a night,

that even the bravest among us
would weep softly in the dark aisles,
catching their difficult breath.

The Children

Lawn chemicals kill, thus
Serrano's infamous "Piss Christ."

Who can now read Saint Mark
where Jesus says, "Whosoever shall offend

one of the little ones that believe in me,
it is better for him that a millstone

were hanged about his neck,
and he were cast into the sea,"

without seeing the dying god
immersed in herbicides and blood?

Where do we think they come from,
the bald children in leukemia wards,

the ones whose cancers eat them alive?
Chicory, milkweed, clover, the diverse lord of nature

now suspended like an embalmed child
in tumors and pollen, poison and urine. . . .

They run across carcinogen greens
in bare feet. We Americans

tax ourselves to pay for this:
thus Serrano's "Piss Christ."

EKG

The last night that the last chemlawn truck
    struck my neighborhood

& the last workers unrolled their hoses & sprayed
    their last rainbows of poison,

under the lurid & mutant grass the last cricket
    died in my ear

& the world's last dandelion heart
    went dead.

Birdhouse

For three or four seasons I'd seen
black-caps trust it, and wrens

in their turn, their twittering young ones
emerging, trying their wings,

being fed, learning to feed themselves,
then departing this acre for other remaining margins

of the crowded world. But,
last week, the living dead visited,

Halloween, and reached it, knocked it out of its silver maple.
Next morning, I lifted its busted gable,

removed petals and stems twined with hair,
feathers softened with rabbit fur,

bits of grass, clover, dandelion heads
dried to the scent of ancient autumn —

no vomit or death smells, no dirt
after seasons of tenants, not even

broken shells or traces of shit,
but clean bedding. Imagine,

hundreds of millions of tons of waste
flushed into the sky each year

in our America. No wonder, last night,
I slept in this house

among birds, the shadows of bombers
flying in and out with water and food,

sweet fume of crickets, intermittent
phosphor of fireflies dropping fuel,

all fused, confused,
as I totter here,

out of nature,
on the dowel below its eye.

N

"Operation Redwing" in the Pacific, 1956. Seventeen
nuclear detonations of large hydrogen weapons.
Colonel Langston Harrison
of the U.S. Air Force's 4926th Squadron
piloted one of twenty-five various aircraft sent in
soon after the explosions
to "make repeated and protracted penetration"
of the mushroom clouds: no special protection,
no procedures for decontamination.
Officially labeled "Human
experiment number 133," under direction
of Los Alamos. Even miles away, even chickens
who turned away & closed their eyes, saw their own
& others' bones. In the clouds, Langston
whistled at the green aura around his B-57,
the lighter green diffusion of sequins within.

Later, limited compensation to civilian populations,
not for the vanished deities of their lagoons,
or their altered genes, or their unborn
or stillborn children, not for proliferation
of cancers for generations, but for eminent domain.

No recognition for most "atomic veterans"
whose records show a few rems of radiation,
who ate 100 — all this foreseen by American technicians
making rational decisions, even warning patriotic skeletons
to remain unknown, even experimental plutonium injections,
the touch of Belsen, engines run
by brains gone into irradiated green,
these lines of translucent skin, this sound begun
at the back of the throat, closed in
with the tip of the tongue,

N.

Trident II: 720,000 Hiroshimas

March 14, 1990 — today, I will not mention what is in my mind.
This day, the year's first robins have arrived.
Brockport has filled with robins, every lawn hosts its pair.
With their chests thrust out, they seem glad to be here.
With their swooping from low limbs to ground,
with their stiff-legged hopping, they seem glad to be here.
Even now, they are pulling worms out of our wet grass.
They eye them sidewise, and dig their beaks in with confidence,
sometimes missing, but often pulling up worms three or four tugs long.

The robins' breasts are not red, but orange mixed with umber.
I'd like to know one from another, and how long they live.
I'd like to know if the same ones return to me each year,
the ones hatched and raised in the bicentennial ash,
the oldest tree in my thoughtful acre,
the one now flowing with March juice,
the one that shelters me so faithfully each summer
whatever is in my mind, the thing that today
I will not mention. . . .

A lifetime ago, in the Bishop Museum in Honolulu,
I saw a chief's cape, thousands of yellow feathers
intricately woven, feathers from now-extinct birds caught
with a glue-like substance spread on limbs, caught
but then released, as I remember the story, or need to remember,
and I would like a cape of umber-orange feathers
from the breasts of robins. Within my cape,
I'd rest in the woods and close my eyes
before the world began. I mean,

as spring light suffused the last trees,
I could hold my knees, and rock, and shed the rain,
and fall asleep, and leave the earth before I knew
what is in my mind. There must be enough robins
for two capes, each woven of hundreds of thousands of feathers.
Will you want this one, or this one?
I'll ask the robins to give me their feathers, to pluck them
from their own breasts and place them in my hands.
I'll be a beggar, my palms open. . . .

Today, I'll do nothing but receive their feathers —
this will be the only thing I'll want to do, or say.
I will arrange the feathers by shades of sunrise to sunset.
I will learn to weave what is not in my mind.
I will spend the coming night under a cape of feathers,
this one, and learn how not to name my fear,
this one. Already, the robins know what is in my mind,
this one, but each pair keeps choosing its nest site
for their eggs' blue flame, this one.

Village Talk During the Massive Build-up of American Arms in the Persian Gulf, August 1990

A dream in which my chest was made of bricks.
I could pull one out, mortar loose around it.
When I reached inside, no moisture, not a drop of blood,
not one tree, fish, snake, or bird.
Five brick surfaces where my heart once beat.
I woke afraid that I had died.

Thoreau said the life in him was like a river.
On Main, Brockport clogs at lights, breaks up, then jams again —
red, green release, yellow caution, red, green release again. . . .
Post office, bank, a tank of gas. Then, chores done,
coffee at the K & K, a big mugful for a buck. Talk
with Kathy & Kevin, Craig, Charlie, Doug, and Squeak.

When it comes my time to die, I'll be afraid, maybe,
but grateful and relieved. After my childhood,
nothing on earth beautiful or charged with love lasted,
except for family and friends. I'll have to remember nature,
where I once lived. Now, in my chest,
that rectangle of dry and empty dark.

Stuff

In the duplication center I xerox a hundred pages
of the usual stuff, you know the stuff.
I xerox maybe a branch's worth, maybe

a small lower branch of Georgia loblolly pine:
evergreen scent of toner, & when I close my eyes,
I see the long needles of light along my branch.

Sometimes, the stuff done, it takes a touch
from next-in-line to break the spell
of xerox, fire, & the wheel.

Pterodactyl Rose

Like you I drive my ten
thousand American miles a year
burning fossil fuels (conversion
to a ton or two of carbon)

but maybe unlike you I peer
into my rear-view mirror imagining air
filling with insects & plants maybe
Triassic dinosaurs

turtles Devonian dragonflies & lilies
such beak & leaf & wing & vine
profusion the past assuming
extinction's shape behind me where I'm going

wild with this prayer of mine,
& longing.

Gods of Vanished Species

At Kwik-Fill, I pump ferns and turtles into my tank.
They'll ride here in my dark until they burn.
Millions of years later, now, our traffic
traverses ancient landscapes, zone by zone,

desert by forest by marsh by swamp until
we sleep. At night, like you, I almost remember
rib-like sprays of cat-tails, pterodactyl eyes of coal,
clouds of insects curving a moonlit shore.

The Real News

When I bought *The Real News* because a human skeleton
had been photographed on the moon,
when I stared at bones in tatters of rags,
the skull leering sidewise into a landscape of craters
on that arid cell of cosmos,

I knew I'd been born a sucker, and, in any case,
over that world and its imagined time,
whatever time it was, our earth still shone, didn't it, familiar
continents in outline where teeming billions still
breathed trees and pure water.

The Body Electric

I flick a switch. The current in my head
divides: DC to India where 800 peasants

can't generate the waste of my one
American home; AC to my children's children,

who must eat my leavings, my light: I see them all
along the future's tungsten filaments as they fade

from rice paddies flaming in the violet sun,
from under the leafless spring cherry boughs of Washington,

DC. AC & DC, the body electric, my brain the eye,
my heart along for the last plush ride on Air Force One.

Night Flight from England

I have finished a third small bottle of whiskey.
I hold the empty bottles, capped by metal,
white roses in their paper labels.

I am flying above ocean, flesh inside metal.
I hold the bottles loosely, thinking, *Lord,
everything is nothing.* I could crush them,

or pass my mind clear through them
under the whale road to England again.
On my wing, one light pulses, or starfish, or star. . . .

Something went wrong somewhere,
or we would not be here. I twist a nozzle
for its stream of oily air.

For now, I'll sleep inside this metal gullet,
dreams fueled by alcohol,
among these hundreds dead, swallowed into time

where whiskey prayer is valid. I can almost,
can't I, smell them here, roses from a bottle,
wild roses by the Little Gidding chapel.

My Sleigh Tonight

I'm here in the aisles among jays & finches
& male golden ring-necked pheasants
& male cardinals imprinted on bags of seed
piled high as my head,

& I'm a little dizzied among the shoppers
counting myself & I'm a little dizzied
by all the dough I've spent & the birds
on these bags trilling & tilting their heads

as though tasting & toasting the niger & millet
& milo & ground yellow corn & wheat
& sunflowers, & I'm a little dizzied
among the holly & mistletoe birds

as muzak mixes the *tsweet, tsweet*
of black-caps & juncos high as my head
in this mallfield scented with some sort
of spice-smelling oil, where I'm a little dizzied

among mourning doves & garden tools among
my feathered pals in the warming aisles
of Christmas under the seedbags & bells
of sprayed berries & suet,

so it's a good thing I find Rudolf guiding
a red tractor where I can sit a while
holding the wheel still, for I'm a little dizzied,
pals, & need to close my eyes a spell. . . .

Fulcrum: The New Poem

It will rope the divided mind, that wild bull
    contagious with lust
    and anthrax.

It will know why farmers kill themselves
    in bankers' barns.
    It will employ facts

that see and hear, paying futures in
    potato eyes,
    cornfield ears.

It will replenish ozone, up there,
    and drink it,
    down here.

It will wade the risen shores of our dying star
    seeding with kelp
    and starfish prayers.

It will unlearn itself to extinction,
    but then
    begin again.

The Global Economy

You've got a dollar. You deposit it in your savings account.
Now you've got a dollar and the bank's got a dollar.

The bank loans a dollar to Joe's Construction. Now you've got
a dollar, the bank's got a dollar, and Joe's got a dollar.

Joe buys a board from Hirohito Lumber. Now Hirohito's got
a dollar, too.

Where did you get your dollar?

How much money is there in the world?

Who's got it?

Where is it?

What happened to all the trees?

Deer

Tar roads & turnpikes, deer
hurtle through darkness
on fenders on hoods on truckbeds
on trailers their eye-strobes
yellow in carlights or walleyed
crimson from neon they lurch
into traffic in cities their bodies

lungless & gutted their numinous
faces their lashes the bucks'
antlers as trees as trophies
dragged from the woods for neighbors
in clusters by trailer by car
touching the fur of the kill calling
deer from the wild, calling *deer*.

Fast Food

I sit at McDonald's eating my fragment of forest.
The snail and slug taste good, the leaves,
the hint of termite and bat, the butterfly trans-

substantiated by steer karma, and mine.
Another pleasure: to breathe distillate of foam
scented with coffee and chemical cream.

Another virtue: groups of us all trained
the same way, millions across America
where we flourish, at present, under the golden arches.

Shoppers' Heaven

Call me Extinction.
I eat lowest on the food chain —
amphibians, algae & plankton,
insects & oxygen.

I shut the lights after the last eco-lecture.
I recycle the unconscious stars.
I forget to load my camera
on purpose. I perfect the cure

for AIDS & cancer, overpopulation,
proliferation of nuclear weapons,
& the mall. Written in black neon,
this legend in my brain:

Welcome, Goodman Heyen, to the communion
of your race. Welcome to Shoppers' Heaven.

The Buffalo

Had the herds roamed the moon,
we could have seen them
in the clear night sky,

rivers of black light
flowing and emptying
into the sea.

The Gift

Because, he said, he didn't want,
because he didn't want them,
because he didn't want them to live,
because he didn't want them to live in poverty,

rainforest Governor Amazonino Mendes distributed
two thousand free chain saws
to his peasant constituents because
he didn't want them to live in poverty,

& it's easy, it's easy for me,
it's easy for me to start this, easy
for me to fill my own chainsaw with gasoline & oil, easy
for me to start this chainsaw snarling, to say

that with his gift Mendes cuts off the feet
of the peasants' children, clear cuts
the family trees of his constituents, easy
for me to speak with a chainsaw tongue

as the trees fall, as the air burns & darkens,
as the forest's blanched soils wash into gullies
because I want peasants to live under trees,
because I want them to live in poverty,

because money means that my nearby mall
carries the perfect gift, & I can easily afford it:
a teak desk set, box inside a box, envelopes,
paper, knife, & a whole roll of U.S. stamps.

Mannikins

Outside my Brockport window, a tangle of windy movement,
but this summer I've missed the *tseep, tseep* of young cardinals
who held unsteadily to twigs in blowing leaflight.
When their parents returned to them with beakfuls of bugs,
the chicks ruffled their feathers, trilled, stretched in excited joy.

From nests where yellowjackets whispered hexagonal cells,
from dunes where beach roses hummed their thorns and blossoms,
from the seed faces of sunflowers, from pasture skullstones,
from brain reefs, from wire fences scrawled with weedy vowels,
from curled lips of lily pads hazed in frogspawn,

from arteries of moles clawing under the dark woods toward words,
from protestant margins where milkweed cracked the edges of asphalt,
from webbed corners beneath breastbone thoughts —
yes, once, but now how do I take what I know, and where?
When, here near the end of my dream, I walk this mall,

eidolons fill my shadows and reflections,
keep me company the others cannot keep me:
plastic generic songbirds perch on aluminum branches,
made to seem to stare at the other dead ones made to tilt
their pelvises into the fashionable future.

Hauge

I've tasted a book by a Norse poet
who has lived his whole life in one place,
an acre of apple trees, his living, his home.
He has come to know where life in them, and him,
bides time even when deep in snow.

These winter mornings, I start my car,
but what's the ignition of apple trees?
Olav Hauge draws back from noise and money,
unlike my own internal combustion engine
which needs armies and navies to sustain it.

Hauge's idea-apples redden like stars forming
among bare branches as he sleeps, even in mid-winter.
I don't trust my life to water and eternity.
I'm an American engine, so out of my way, Hauge,
you with your universe of apple trees.

A Jar

Each noon, at the construction site around the corner
from my own wooded suburban acre,
I checked progress: the bigger trees — almost all ash,
a few maple, one white oak — chainsawed, dragged out
by dozer and chain; then dozer back in for clearing brush;

then dozer, backhoe, and ten-ton roller to cut
foundation-, drainage-, and sewer-pipe patterns
into subsoil and clay, to pack dirt so it would never shift.
Day by day, in drizzle or shower, hot sun
or one sudden out-of-season jet stream shift to chill,

the men widened the site's geometric margins
to where, in one corner, piles of trucked-in sand
diminished a twenty-foot puddle filled for weeks
with thousands of tadpoles just beginning
to grow legs and lose their tails. The time would come,

of course, to fill this last swale. Meanwhile,
the polliwog population prospered in this luke-warm
algae-sweetened pond of their world. . . .
And then was gone, all at once, their birthplace levelled
with sand and a few inches of good topsoil

over which we walked. That was that, except
for this, the one thing, the thing in itself:
how, at about this time, our species began to document
amphibians' disappearance across the globe;
how marshes and swamps were growing silent;

and how, an actor in our sentimental elegy, one worker
placed in his tool chest to take home at quitting time
a jar filled with muddy water and a host of tadpoles,
little blips of sperm-shaped black light.
To catch them, he must have knelt and cupped them in his palms.

Jersey

In the old days before instant replays my Pop
jumped up between the 14th and 15th rounds for a beer
and missed a wicked knockout, Jersey Joe Walcott over
I don't remember. Jersey Joe, of course, was happy,
Pop pissed he'd missed a chopping overhand right
that would have stunned a steer.

To bowl his natural hook, Pop spit in his palm,
then chalked up. When his ball crossed over
out of the right hand Brooklyn groove to the Jersey side,
he sometimes struck, sometimes split, but always
glared at his hand, disgusted, muttering "goddamn
Jersey, stop throwing those goddamn Jerseys."

I know a novelist, Madison Smartt Bell, one of the roughs
sometimes abashed by his own education who, when pressed,
says he attended a small college in New Jersey.
You know the place, made famous by Einstein, Bill Bradley,
and Brooke Shields who, as she studied there, kept a journal
published in installments in *TV Guide*: fashions and film trips.

The first book on Bradley was John McFee's
A Sense of Where It Is, his title explaining
how to score when you can't see a target,
the basket when your back's to it, e.g.
"Dollar Bill" has the first buck he ever made, they say,
and ran the defense into tough blind-side picks, e.g.

We still sense where it is, as though, if we changed,
pastures would regenerate, and, before too late, forests,
that world other-than-only-ourselves. Jersey Joe Einstein says
we can't miss getting there from here, but we will, unless
like this: dreaming America, take a deep mind's breath, head
south along the Jersey shore, and hook a left.

(for Joyce Carol Oates)

Off the Hamptons

At night,
off the Hamptons,
the sky deceives with stars
long burnt out,

shellfish poachers
dig the forbidden waters
off the duck farms,
play hide-and-seek

with lawmen who slide
over the marshes in flat boats
like fish at the ocean's bottom,
one white ray of an eye

mounted on their foreheads.
Here the waters are poison,
the clams thick as diamonds
in the fables of lost mines.

Bark City Broadway

Here I'm an iron spike while
city chainsaws fume closer that never
cared this tree listened to its god
of sunlight & ocean mists before

Jesus I remember forge & flame
if I could disappear in heartwood
but I am thought-suffused & dumb
inside this foot-thick bark

of sorrel & limos & green cathedral
windows & sorrow as nearing teeth
snarl their non-sustainable speech
of mannikins & need & money's worth

& muscle & root & branch & sky
& gems & sap & needles & whores
& seedlings & children & gospel & eye I
can't cross the pavement forest floor

but wait as defensive weapon here
for when my time will come to maim
the corporate victim dying to clear
this last redwood by quitting time.

Radical American Heartwood Breakdown Amulet Prayer

Yes, we'll put people out of work
when we stop razing the last old-growth forests,
sequoia that trembled in mist when Christ died on the cross,

but we put people out of work
when we shut down that kingdom of cordwood,
Auschwitz. Let forest *SS* murderers wither under the holy trees.

Trees

I caught the one man I hate
at the back of my acre where he'd gouged two holes.
He had two honey-locust saplings
in their yellow-green spring trill and tinge

ready to set. "Bastard," I yelled,
"what do you think you are?"
I had a shovel in my hands, and swung it.
He lay down, slowly, his arms crossed on his chest. . . .

The trees were in their places, antennae sweeping low
to pull soil into their holes. As I do, here?
Do I remember that I lay myself beside him? . . .

I remember trees, all summer, honey-amber,
the locusts' green, insistent speech
as I stared upward through their wings.

Emancipation Proclamation

Whereas it minds its own business
& lives in its one place so faithfully
& its trunk supports us when we lean against it
& its branches remind us of how we think

Whereas it keeps no bank account but hoards carbon
& does not discriminate between starlings & robins
& provides free housing for insects & squirrels
& lifts its heartwood grave into the air

Whereas it holds our firmament in place
& writes underground gospel with its roots
& whispers us oxygen with its leaves
& may not survive its new climate of ultraviolet

We the people for ourselves & our children
necessarily proclaim this tree
free from commerce & belonging to itself
as long as it & we shall live.

The Swamp

Stretched out underwater, neck telescoped forward,
smelling the spring mud as though just waking,
behemoth walked in a drowse. Braced myself,

hauled it in two pulls by its fat tail to shore
where it blinked and shut itself off to such nonsense,
withdrew its neck to wait out whatever. . . .

Noticed a leech necklace, glints of topaz in its eyes,
nostrils protruding upward so it could breathe while
hidden in muck with its maw open,

its pretty pink inviting tongue wiggling.
Fed it a stick: it struck in a hiss and snapped it.
Thought of creatures it had eaten —

even an adult blue heron piteously broken,
leg by wing, at last dragged down in mid-cry.
Wanted to end this snapper and all its children

in their primitive armor, wanted to boil it,
eat its heart, digest it at leisure in a trance of bliss
in my own top-of-the-food-chain arrogance, . . .

but if we rid the world of snappers, would mosquitos cloud
when herons ate all frogs? Was there balance here,
or have we come too far filling in wetlands, forcing

every last heron into the snapper's jaws? Yearned
to knife its voracious brain to the ground,
but wanted to do the precarious right thing, you understand. . . .

In the end, wouldn't act alone. Looped a wire
around its shell, tied it to a tree with enough play
so it could just reach water or climb ashore. . . .

We've all summer to decide. If you want me to,
I'll ax its ugly bejeweled head off, or let it loose.
Listen to the swamp, and let me know.

Matrix

When I was a boy,
I found a mutilated turtle
emerging from mud.
Something, when it was young,
had broken its shell
almost in half,
but the shell,
as though welded with glossy solder,
had mended;
something had chewed
its back legs to the joints,
but its stumps were hard.
How did you survive,
I asked it,
but it was mute, still half adream
from its winter sleep.
I spoke to it,
warmed it in my boy's hands,
but it boxed itself up. . . .

For some time
after her mastectomy,
weeks of hospital and chemotherapy,
my wife woke toward me
in slow spirals,
as though from ether,
unsure of where we were
and how we'd live
in our new matrix
of scar and fear.
But it was April, again.
In windows before us,
as we changed her dressings,
the days rained, and warmed.
One morning, I pressed my lips
to her chest until, at last,
she believed,
and opened up to me,
our answers so slow to come
that came.

Looking Away

At the edge of this Brockport acre, an acorn has sprouted.
Our neighborhood is all ash, maple, hybrid ornamentals,
but here is the great tree itself, three inches high, poised within
marginal diffusion of grasses and goldenrod,
Queen Anne's lace, September's purple aster.
To mark it, I drove a stake beside it. I'll cover it
with leaves and wire for a winter or three,
until it doesn't need me.

Last night, home late from a waste of drinking and talk,
lungs and clothes filled with others' smoke,
I walked outside beside the room where my wife was waiting,
and kept walking. I found the stake and could see,
the way we see in darkness,
the way we see when we look away,
the newborn tree sheathed in a silver aura
within the cosmos of its neighbors. . . .

These days, when pain allows, she sleeps on her left side,
her heart side, her good side, looking away.
I knelt for god to let her live
here in the prayer-wheels
of the several churches along Main beyond the waters
of the old Canal in which I float these words and look away
for hundreds of years from now. And now, for once, beyond reason,
the mourning voices of doves in the oak's leaves, and peace.

Elmwood

Not hard, just
a missed tap
    while setting a wedge,
but blood pooled

at the base of my thumbnail,
blotted the pale
    stationary
half-

moon that never
rises, then
    gradually
floated upward,

a red sunrise
within that world.
    Months later,
after my slow staring,

it reached
the outer rim until,
    day by day,
I scraped it away

until that sky
flowed pink, clear,
    the dead elms
drying for fire

in the mind's
concentrated kiln-
    like stutter, here,
as I remember

nature, that moon's
reflection, that sun's
    hovering,
blood running

over rapids
like woodsmoke, the clouds
    like elmleaves
between.

Elmwood. Swirls of grain.
Resists splitting.
    Won't split, won't,
but will.

Yellowjackets

1.

Two months before,
　　I'd let the meadow grow.
　　　　Now, I leaned on my scythe again.
　　Brockport's August sun

glimmered a just-
　　visible blue in pods
　　　　of chest-high thistles

(I knew that painted ladies favored these,
　　as monarchs did the now-poised
　　　　succulent milkweed for their eggs)

and clover and Queen Anne's lace
　　bloomed with meadow's
　　　　basic, ragged, profuse,
　　adjectival beauty.

2.

I spared the meadow, and was lucky:
　　a few feet away, yellowjackets
　　　　streamed into two holes

under a hummock's ledge; others
　　veered upward and outward again
　　　　past my face to their fields of pollen.

3.

I returned last evening
　　for the spraying and burning —
　　　　first the arc of deadly fluid
　　from my fingertip,
then the gas-soaked rags flaming

above the wasps' buried comb.
　　Lit gold by the falling sun,
　　　　the last workers to return
　　circled their smoldering,
hoed-up home. . . .

4.

He came toward me, and I loved him,
could hold his hands, could kiss him,
his torso and limbs flesh like my own son's,
his neck the same slim neck I have known,

but this one's face was cells, a comb
running with honey. When I stared,
I saw yellowjackets flying
into his two black pupils

into their meadow again.
    "This is the only way in,"
he said, as his pupils widened.

Inside, a few whose wings
ignited in the falling sun
still circled a child who smoldered
and wept honey light

into the meadow's grasses.
    Inside him, kneeling beside him, I
who had killed him tried to help him.

5.

If my son's eyes opened into meadow
    where wasps circled above a dead boy
        weeping honey, this was my dream, yes,
    but the land is our child,
and everyman's theta-waves scan

for the something hidden, perfect hexagonal cells
    where the newborn hum
        below our hearing, the random-patterned broken
    circling of those returning
to the underground forms of the world. This is the music

that plays as we sleep,
    melody gathering, echoing
        all we should have known. The yellowjackets wait
    for human eyes to widen, when they will fly in,
where they will live, again.

The Bargain

We stood in spikes of blowing goldenrod,
in clumps of clover where fat bees bumbled for pollen,
but my friend's eyes were closed,
for he had reached a placelessness beyond dimension. . . .

The poet Jack Gilbert has written,
"Every wise man I met in Asia warned me against caring,
explained how everything I loved would get old,
or be taken away, and I would suffer.

"I tried to explain what a bargain it is. . . ."
What a bargain it is, the billion-winged field to keep,
to lose, Chien-Ping and I, he where no wind blows,
I where a grasshopper clings to my wristhairs.

If there are times that add to our store of time,
then this, if there is time at all.
I remember that just before returning, Chien-Ping swayed,
how he had to clear his throat before speaking. . . .

There, here, after our out-of-mind-and-body travel,
this bargain, the way we keep returning to an earth
drifting six or eight hundred miles a second
into a vast stardark vacuum,

such god-forsaken and god-suffused emptiness
and fullness, black holes and pollen.

Crickets

Evenings, where lawns are not sprayed with poisons,
you can still hear the crickets,
you can still see lightning bugs signalling,

look, a yellowgreen strobe under the trees,
but gone, but there again, sometimes
in the same spot, and sometimes not,

as the tiny purveyors of phosphor
drift past our houses, looking
for one another, and the crickets,

crickets, crickets, the ones that still
have their legs, keep scraping them together,
listen, maybe for the last time on earth, listen. . . .

William Heyen's poems have appeared in more than a hundred periodicals, including *The New Yorker, Harper's, TriQuarterly, Poetry,* and *American Poetry Review.* His honors include two fellowships from the National Endowment for the Arts, the John Simon Guggenheim Fellowship in Poetry, the Eunice Tietjens Memorial Prize from *Poetry* magazine, and the Witter Bynner Prize for Poetry from the American Academy and Institute of Arts and Letters. Mr. Heyen's previous books include **Depth of Field, Long Island Light, Lord Dragonfly,** and **The Chestnut Rain.** His next three volumes of poetry, a second edition of **Erika: Poems of the Holocaust, Ribbons: The Gulf War — A Poem,** and **The Host: Selected Poems, 1965-1990,** are forthcoming from his publisher, Time Being Books of St. Louis, Missouri. Mr. Heyen is currently Professor of English and Poet in Residence at the State University of New York College at Brockport.

Also available from **Time Being Books**

LOUIS DANIEL BRODSKY
You Can't Go Back, Exactly
The Thorough Earth
Four and Twenty Blackbirds Soaring
Mississippi Vistas: Volume One of *A Mississippi Trilogy*
Forever, for Now: Poems for a Later Love
Mistress Mississippi: Volume Two of *A Mississippi Trilogy*
A Gleam in the Eye: Poems for a First Baby
  Volume One of *A Pentalogy of Childhood*

WILLIAM HEYEN
Erika: Poems of the Holocaust

LOUIS DANIEL BRODSKY and WILLIAM HEYEN
Falling from Heaven: Holocaust Poems of a Jew and a Gentile

Please call or write for a free catalog.

TIME BEING BOOKS
POETRY IN SIGHT AND SOUND
Saint Louis, Missouri

10411 Clayton Road • Suite 208
St. Louis, Missouri 63131
(314) 432-1771

TO ORDER TOLL-FREE
(800) 331-6605 Monday through Friday, 8 a.m. to 4 p.m. Central time
FAX: (314) 432-7939